Pre-Publication Critics' Reviews, Fan Mail and Anonymous Death Threats

"This is the Far Side of Maine. It is awful. I loved it."
        Margaret Chaste Smith

"I read every word. I couldn't put it down. The publisher held me at gunpoint."
        The Boston Sunday Globule

"You can swiftly tell that the authors don't know the first thing about building a post and beam jacuzzi bath."
        New Mainers Times

"When will our do-nothing wimp of a governor invoke his constituted powers and hang these cheap scribblers?"
        Maine Sunday Cardiogram

"If any book ever deserved burning!"
        Maine Civil Liberties Congress

"Rest assured that the Nuclear Power Cartels, the White Rulers in South Africa, the Terror Regime in Chile, the Land Rapers here in Maine are the ultimate beneficiaries of this brand of humor."
        Democratic Terrorists of Maine

"We're going to take you for every cent you got."
        Special Task Force of the Maine Legal Association

God's Country Next Exit

How to Survive in the New Maine

Pictures by George Hughes

Words by Charles McAleer

 Lance Tapley, Publisher

Text copyright ©1986 by Charles McAleer.

Cartoons copyright ©1986 by George Hughes.

All rights reserved.

No part of this book may be reproduced or transmitted in any form or by any means, electronic or mechanical, including photocopying, recording, or by any information storage and retrieval system, without the written permission of the publisher, except by a reviewer quoting brief passages in a magazine, newspaper or broadcast. Address inquiries to Lance Tapley, Publisher, P.O. Box 2439, Augusta, Maine 04330.

Printed in the United States of America

Second printing

With special thanks to Jon Stamell

Library of Congress Cataloging-in-Publication Data

Hughes, George, 1943-
   God's country next exit.

   1. Maine—Social life and customs—Anecdotes, facetiae, satire, etc. 2. Maine—Social life and customs—Caricatures and cartoons. 3. American wit and humor, Pictorial. I. McAleer, Charles, 1949-
II. Title.
F19.6.H84   1986   974.1'043   86-23152
ISBN 0-912769-09-2

CONTENTS

So You Think You Belong in Maine?	7
Tips, Pointers, Do's, Don't's and Handle-with-Cares in Maine Etiquette	15
The Most Important Recent Maine Court Decisions and Why They're Better Than Going to the Movies	18
The Maine Experience as Told by the People Who Live It Daily	22
A Compendium of Maine Country Lore, Trivia, Advice, and Outright Falsehoods	26
Trying to Make Sense of the Maine Driver	30
Who It Pays to Collide with	32
The Official Maine Values, Attitude and Lifestyles Survey	38
From *The Collectors' Souvenir Edition of Maine Pornography*	41
Have You Been Paying Attention?	46
Authentic Down-Home, Down-East Parlor Games	52
Sailing the Maine Coast	58
A Rainy Day in Maine	64
What Color Are Your Food Stamps?	68
Who Makes What in Maine	72
Arts Diary	76
Examples of Acceptable and Unacceptable Names for Maine People	79
The Most Important Referendum Question to be Put Before the People of Maine in the History of The World	82
Suggestions for Further Reading	86

So You Think You Belong in Maine?

A Self-Scoring Maine Lifestyle Aptitude Test

turn to page 12 to score your answers

1. After years of dreaming and talking, the two of you finally make the big move and quit the big city for a small, midcoastal Maine community. Intelligently aware of the unwritten Maine social code, you don't push yourselves forward and are content to wait for the locals to make the first overtures. Before long your discretion pays off. Your nearest neighbors, who live a mile down the road, invite you over for a barbecue supper. It doesn't take long to break the ice, and before the second six-pack you're congratulating yourselves on how well the evening's going. Eventually your host rises, explaining it's time "to kill the fatted calf." You naturally offer to lend a hand with the fire or whatever. You follow him out behind his house, where you see a cow tethered to a chopping block. Your host offers you an axe, saying: "Guest's choice. Want to carve her up or hold her still?" You should:

   A) Suddenly remember you left the water running in your swimming pool.

   B) Run home and fetch your new chain saw, which you're just dying to try out anyway.

   C) Ask if by any chance you could have moose instead.

2. One of your major motives in moving to Maine was to give your children a healthy place to grow up. The problem is your eldest daughter. She misses her friends back at her old high school and doesn't seem to be making any new ones. You're relieved when one day she excitedly tells you about Willard, two

years ahead of her, who asked her out for Saturday afternoon. You happily give your permission. But come Saturday, your first impression of Willard isn't exactly sterling. He pulls a rusty Luger out of his jacket and tells you that your daughter and he have a rendezvous at the dump to shoot some rats. You feel you can't let him do this with your daughter, but you've read all of Stephen King's books and know how dangerous Maine pride can be when offended. So you:

A) Ask to see the gun and then shoot him.

B) Offer him your BMW if he'll go away.

C) Make a pass at him.

3. Having run out of outlet stores to send your summer guests to, you take them for a short sail in your boat. Nothing adventurous—you gauge correctly that, to them, running out of brie while in their hot tub would qualify as a major epic of endurance on the high seas. Things are going smoothly; they are gurgling about whatever visitors like to gurgle about, and you don't have to talk to them because everybody knows that Maine people are permitted to sit there like dead fish if they want to. But, while you're returning to your mooring, one of them grabs a lobster buoy and hauls it in, exclaiming that lobster would be just the thing for dinner that night. Beaming, he holds up a semidisguised surplus naval mine which the rightful owner of the trap installed to discourage just such thefts. As your eyes travel between the mine and the silly ass who thinks he's holding a fresh Maine lobster, you very calmly drawl that:

A) He should throw it back because it's too small.

B) He should hang onto it until you can return with a camera.

C) He should eat it raw like the natives do.

4. To the horror of your upper-middle-class parents in Long Island, when you graduated from college you announced you were going to Maine and live in a tar-paper shack, dig for clams, and write poetry. That was fifteen years ago, and you've kept your word—about the shack and the clams anyway. Meanwhile, your brother who works on Wall Street has become very successful and incredibly obnoxious. Your sister, who is some kind of lawyer in D.C., is even a bigger jerk. At Christmas when you all get together, it's become a yearly tradition for the whole lot of them to bug you about goofing off in Maine instead of getting a real job. You're tired of it, so this year you decide to:

A) Put on your old prep-school blazer, twist your face into your most urbane smile, and pick up the whole turkey with your bare hands and eat it.

B) Invite them all to Maine; when they arrive, serve them red-tide clams.

C) Disinherit them.

5. Your neighbor seems the pure embodiment of the Maine lifestyle. Independent, works his own small but solvent farm, puts on no airs, and, above all, really practices self-sufficiency. In contrast, you and your spouse drive to your jobs in matching Saabs with bumper stickers declaring that you brake for whales, have a Calvin Klein woodstove, and send your cat to a top-notch prep school. But like many other ex-60s types, the flame of social commitment still smolders within you. You think nuclear power is really yucky, for example. When one day your neighbor casually mentions that he is building his own nuclear power plant behind his woodshed, you know something very important has just been put on the line, something you can't walk away from this time. You and your spouse talk it over and:

A) Decide to send over some sushi with the worms still inside.

B) Decide to use your solar collector as a giant magnifying glass and burn his nuke to the ground.

C) Decide to circulate a rumor that your neighbor is building summer-resort condominiums.

So You Think You Belong in Maine?

Scoring Your Answers

continued from page 10

1. *Answer A:* What if he started sending his dirty old cows over to your swimming pool anytime they were thirsty? Score yourself 0 points.

   Answer B: Bulls eye! Give yourself 2 points. Not only have you sent him a signal that you aren't some sissy-pants from the city, but you've even taught him a new way to deal with an old chore.

   Answer C: Score 1 point. While you might have deftly headed off the immediate crisis, on the other hand you might have a neighbor here who hadn't won in the moose lottery—and this might be a sore point to bring up.

2. *Answer A:* 0 points. He doubtless has brothers you'd have to reckon with.

   Answer B: Nice try. But as a rule of thumb the true Mainer doesn't have much use for a foreign car, particularly if the rear window is too small for a gun rack. 1 point.

   Answer C: Score yourself 2 points if you're female; 200 if you're male.

3. *Answer A:* 0 points. You don't really want these people around next year, do you?

Answer B: 2 points. This is a good idea, particularly if you have a very, very long-range telephoto lens.

Answer C: 1 point. Yes, this is an opportunity to create an instant, classic piece of Down East folklore ("Did you hear the one about the tourist on the coast with a case of indigestion people heard as far away as Fort Kent?"), but there are already hundreds of bean-supper jokes on similar themes.

4. *Answer A:* Yeah, sounds like fun. 2 points if you get some gravy on your father's Yale beanie.

   Answer B: Zip points. The trouble with this idea is that people in your family's social class are notorious for consuming massive quantities of alcohol daily. Consequently, their digestive tracts are perfectly immune to most forms of food poisoning and bacteriological warfare.

   Answer C: Give yourself a big 10. Why didn't you say you had become a big-time condo developer?

5. *Answer A:* 0 points. You've misread Maine natives. He'd probably use it as window caulking.

   Answer B: Okay, 2 points. But you had better do it before he loads it up, or you'll have a Chernobyl next door.

   Answer C: Deduct 5 points. Many Maine people think condos are a great idea. Even better than a nuke, and there's certainly more money to be made with them.

Tips, Pointers, Do's, Don't's, and Handle-with-Cares in Maine Etiquette

1. If by good fortune you are invited by a Maine family into their home, bring a small but meaningful gift such as a $5.00 bill.

2. Acceptable anniversary gifts: 1st anniversary, tube of Bondo; 5th, plaid ice chest; 10th, checked polyester table linen (in-door/out-door); 25th, 50-pound bag of loam; 50th, bus tickets to Florida.

3. In many places asking for the "little boy's" or "little girl's" room means you have come to arrange a marriage with the son or daughter of the house.

4. The days when you could trade colored glass, pretty beads, and old skins at Maine's factory outlets are all but over. Especially, don't try it at L.L. Bean. They've become rather snotty.

5. If in deer-hunting season you have the misfortune to shoot a hunter unknown to you personally, local custom dictates that you write a brief note of regret to the deceased's family in which you offer to get a deer for them.

6. The use of Parisian French words and expressions is frowned upon among the higher classes of Maine people. Take pains to pronounce Yves St. Laurent as "Yips Sand Lawrence." When you go shopping, you'll receive more attentive service.

7. In public eating places, don't belch. This is by tradition the prerogative of regular customers.

8. Always let the phone ring at least 10 minutes before you answer. It is important not to seem too much in a hurry.

9. It is thought the height of boorishness by Maine people for someone to attempt to tell them anything.

10. You can judge the kind of restaurant by observing whether the men or the women wear hats while eating.

11. Women only: If you sense you're in imminent danger of being "picked up" at a bar or restaurant, throw your head back and loudly gargle whatever drink is at hand. This is a real turn-off to Maine men.

12. If you must cross private property, take pains to shut the gate behind you, crouch low, and run like hell.

13. Never ask your host where he bought the (moose, deer, wildcat, etc.) head hanging in his den.

14. The practice of giving flowers is unknown outside of the larger cities. The traditional token of affection or esteem is a load of fill.

15. When you are taken home by your Maine-born fiancée to meet the family you'll make a good impression by counting to fifty silently each time before you speak.

16. Don't wear loud, vulgar clothing except during deer-hunting season.

17. More ways to advertise that you're not from Maine: wearing shorts and extremely warm Icelandic sweaters at the same time, or Australian Army surplus jungle clothes, or T-shirts which say that you're in the state of Maine.

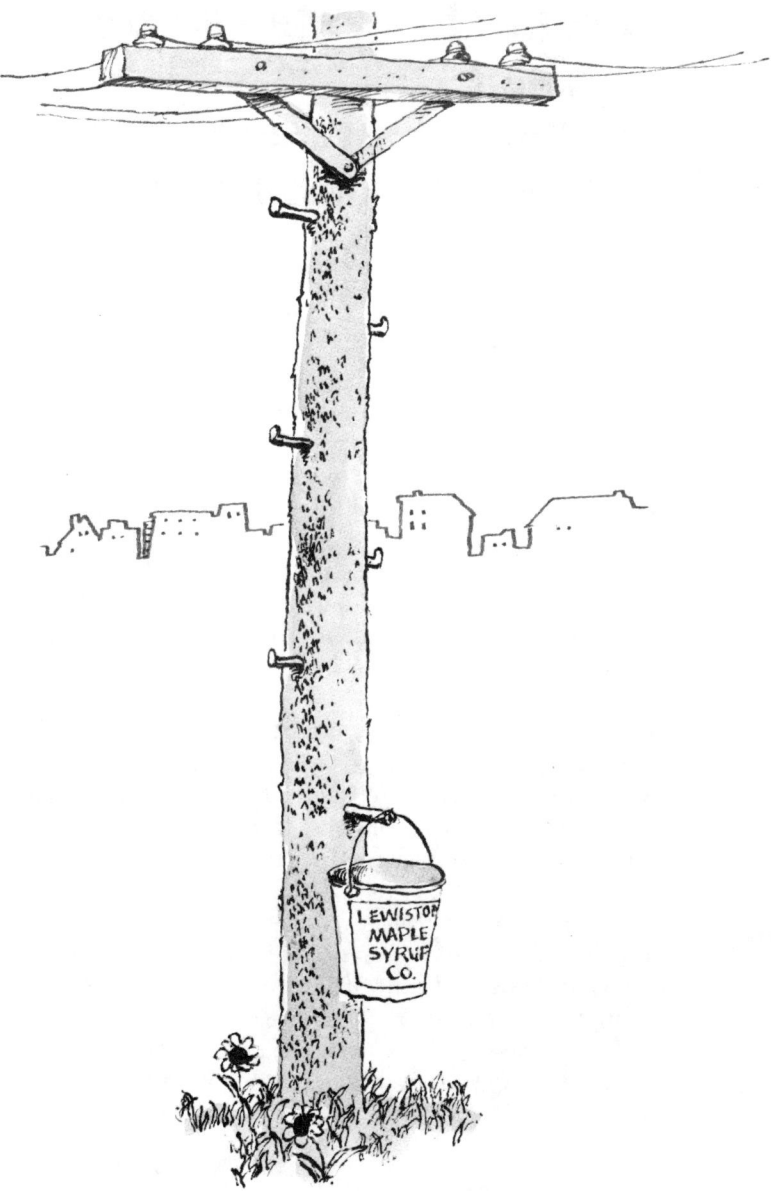

The Most Important Recent Maine Court Decisions and Why They're Better Than Going to the Movies

It has been reported that in Maine's principal city, Portland, the ratio of lawyers to honest, gainfully employed citizens is second only to that in Washington, D.C. Not unnaturally, the sheer density of the profession has had a profound influence on the evolution of Maine law, tending to make it rather complex. Nor should economics be ignored in assessing how Maine law has been created. Some of Maine's lawyers are quite affluent. Sadly, however, all too many of their colleagues are forced into the pursuit of ambulances in hopes of catching the occasional loose tailpipe or hubcap. Nevertheless, in spite of these negative influences, the law has managed to retain a strong core of the common sense, practicality, humanity, and native wit which are Maine's very essence, as the following court decisions attest:

Abortion. In a recent landmark decision, the state's Highest Court absolutely refused to extend freedom of choice to a pregnant lobster, apparently fearing the long-term adverse effects on tourism if shellfish, fish, chickens, cows, deer, and other Maine delicacies were granted reproductive choice.[1]

Division of Property in Divorce Settlements. No issue has proven as vexing to Maine courts as the equitable division of joint property when a husband and wife seek a divorce. Apparently finding little to recommend in the long, costly legal procedures developed in other states, the courts here prefer to make settlements on the basis of such traditional games of skill or luck as chain-saw dueling.[2]

Father's Right to Custody. Firmly turning their backs on the many, many cases nationwide that speak directly to this issue,[3] Maine's courts have preferred to be guided by a vaguely relevant local case[4] in which the plaintiff, Hummer, refused to return an empty water-cooler bottle to the Rockland Bottled Water Company, having gone mad and come to believe the bottle to be in reality his infant son and himself the natural mother. The issue came down to who could provide it with a better home environment, and the High Court decided in favor of the plaintiff on the grounds of his new, self-cleaning refrigerator. Rockland was, however, given visiting rights every other weekend.

Indecent Exposure—"The Union Suit Test." Carefully distinguishing between Maine's traditional long woolen undergarment, which has many buttons down the front, and such foreign attire as boxer shorts, jockey shorts, and skimpy black briefs, the Superior Court held that in light of the time required to unfasten the former, the allegedly outraged spectators in one case were, on the contrary, salivating voyeurs, and the court ordered that their eyeglasses be burned in public.[5] But in a similar case heard next door at the barber shop, compelling evidence was presented that certain judges in the backwoods knowingly and premeditatedly went around naked under their robes in summer. As a result, the U.S. Circuit Court of Appeals called these judges all kinds of four-letter words in Latin and ordered them fifty velcro fig leaves from L.L. Bean forthwith.[6]

Palimony. Maine courts have tended to look harshly upon the claims by "companions" to a share of deceaseds' estates. Learned Justice Bigfoot elegantly summarized the various complex legal and moral issues involved when he declared: "I want that damn bimbo on the next bus to Boston."[7]

Weird Lawsuits. Plaintiff visited state with his family and in-laws, all of whom in the course of the trip he bound, gagged, and dropped off at the Lewiston Bus Station, having carefully wrapped them in brown shipping paper. Subsequently, on the advice of his attorney, he brought suit against the State of Maine, demanding that it pay the costs incurred in shipping them back home to Ohio. He alleged that the "Vacationland" on Maine license plates constituted an unconditional obligation on the part of the state to ensure that his stay in Maine would be pleasurable, when in fact it was boring, depressing, and caused him to hear voices bidding him to do bizarre things. The Supreme Judicial Court of Maine concurred, adding that they heard voices all the time.[8]

Look Up These Footnotes and You'll Know as Much Law as Some Lawyers in Maine. Maybe More.

[1]*State v. Flipper.*

[2]*Savage v. Savage.*

[3]See, for example, California's *Cootie v. Cootie.*

[4]*Hummer v. the Rockland Bottled Water Company.*

[5]*State v. Boaner.*

[6]*People v. Everybody Else.*

[7]*Trixi v. Estate of Walter S. Banger.*

[8]*Bjerko v. State.*

"Well, I'll admit it does have something to say about the coast."

The Maine Experience as Told by the People Who Live It Daily

Helen, self-employed, Moosehorn Corners: "My husband Roy and I run a beauty salon and car body shop. Business is pretty good, and when I have to do one of those new hair-do's I can always borrow his blow torch, and he borrows my curlers when he puts on Bondo. I hoped our sons would take over the business someday, but the oldest moved out of state and got a job as a dog, and last week the other wrote he's the new premier of Russia. He says he will try and send some money."

Walter, elementeery skul teecher in Arrostik cowty: "I'm weerried about the kids in my clas. They dont do there lesions, and wen I tri to tel them sumfing they laf and gigel. My gurlfreend is a ten eared perfesser at the Univarsity and sez they shood higher me."

Marty, former New York stockbroker, now a freelance mortician in Bar Harbor: "No doubt about it, Maine was a pretty drastic change of scene for me. No, I don't look back, not really. My ex-wife was here the other day from New York, so we talked over old times, had a glass of wine, laughed together, cried together, and she got to talking about how much money she was making. I pickled her with enough embalming fluid to stand her up in the Macy's parade . . . you're not from the police, are you?"

Carolyn, Portland-based sales executive, moonlights as a roofer: "All in all, I'd say my careers are strongly in a positive-trajectory mode. I basically feel good about the overall Maine achievement-matrix for women. I definitely feel I can input those I work with and am encouraged to run with the ball up the flag pole whenever I want to. As for the perks of living in Maine, whoever thought up the idea of time-sharing running shoes can have this working girl's phone number anytime he wants!"

Dell and Barney, coastal real-estate developers: "Don't expect us to go all a-weeping and tearing our hair out because Maine is getting developed. It belonged lock, stock, and barrel to rich out-of-state millionaires anyway. Why, when we were growing up they'd hire the fishing fleet to sail by at such-and-such a time just so their guests could take snapshots. And this was seventy-five miles inland . . ."

Frank, poet and odd-jobber around Portland: "I moved to Maine because I wanted a sane environment for serious writing. But the "f" and "u" keys on my typewriter got worn out, and I couldn't afford to repair it . . . Did you know there's some rich guy up the coast who's offering $10,000 to the person who writes the best 30,000-line heroic epic poem in praise of nuclear power plants? I wonder if it has to rhyme . . ."

Franklin, retired banker: "People in Maine just don't know what's happening. They don't want to know. There is absolutely no doubt in my mind that international Jews are in cahoots with the Communists to assassinate Maine's fish and game wardens and replace them with their own agents . . . How come Maine natives just don't see these things?"

Vern, lobsterman and certified historic monument: "Whenever I came to unload my catch at the wharf the tourists would come and point those long cameras at me, and as it eventually became highly perturbing, I resolved to play them a little Maine joke which my father taught me long, long before many of you were ever born. Accordingly, one day I reached deep into my trousers . . . Well, all the cameras stopped clicking."

"One more time... why did you cross the road?"

"Your sticker's out of date."

A Compendium of Maine Country Lore, Trivia, Advice, and Outright Falsehoods

- To remove a stain in an article of clothing, take a pair of clippers or a sharp knife and carefully cut out the discolored area.

- Country people believe that on moonless summer nights the frogs in the surrounding ponds dispense free advice concerning the stock market.

- The great blue heron, that most graceful and delicate of birds which has figured in legends and folklore, is known in Maine by this evocative, poetic name: shitpoke.

- An undertaker from the town of Milo is the inventor of stuttering.

- The famous composer Ludwig von Beethoven never once set foot in Maine during his entire life.

- In Maine you can paint insects to resemble small lobsters and sell them to the tourists.

- Even the largest of mooses will run away in utter panic at the sight of a bedroom slipper, especially one with a plaid interior.

- The first "talkie" movie to arrive in Maine was "Jaws" in 1979.

- Resourceful Maine housewives will often collect lumps of tar off the road on a hot summer day and serve them as homemade fudge in roadside stands to the tourists.

- The legendary American inventor Thomas Alva Edison gave the first public demonstration of electricity's vast potential when he was hired by the state to electrocute the entire population of Bangor for tax delinquency.

- The late, infamous Soviet dictator Joseph Stalin would fall to the floor shrieking and would rend people's shoes apart with his bare teeth at the mere mention of the name "Maine."

- By tradition dating back to colonial days, people born with two left feet are exempted from paying their debts and upon their twenty-first birthday are given high political office.

- You can keep a car warm through the coldest of Maine winter nights by keeping it some place warm.

- An old farm remedy for a cold is to swallow a small glass of kerosene and then a burning wooden match.

- When the old sea captains' wives spied their husbands' ships returning after a long voyage, they would quickly disguise their gentlemen callers as dogs, cats, parrots and other familiar household pets.

- An old-time Maine farmers' trick: If you want to make certain your dog won't ever chase cars, tie one end of a stout cord around his neck and the other to the front bumper of your car, then run him over once or twice.

- When a Maine youth wants a girl to marry him, he will first make himself as charming as possible by hiring a substitute from Boston.

- The late, infamous German dictator Adolf Hitler would fall to the floor shrieking and would rend people's shoes apart with his bare teeth at the mere mention of the name "Maine."

- Bothered by mosquitoes? An old fishermen's method for dealing with all small, pesky insects is to capture them between thumb and forefinger and squeeze firmly.

- A quaint, old-time custom which survives to this day in many Maine communities: telephoning restaurants under a false name and making dinner reservations for twenty-seven people.

- To this day nobody in Maine can spell Masachusetts. And they're proud of it.

- When a Piscataquis County resident hears a jet aircraft loudly flying overhead, he will take off his hat and observe to his companions: "Aiyee . . . iron bird in the sky!"

- The late, infamous Haitian dictator Papa Doc Duvalier would fall to the floor shrieking and would rend people's shoes apart with his bare teeth at the mere mention of the name "Maine."

- Country folk firmly believe that falling off a ladder means bad luck.

Trying to Make Sense of the Maine Driver

Getting from point A to point B in Maine with any degree of efficiency is partly a matter of luck and partly a matter of common sense. But, as veteran drivers will testify, it's mostly a matter of steadfastly pretending that you're deaf and blind every time you get behind the wheel. But you say: "If I close my eyes, I'll miss out on all the stuff I live in Maine for!" Relax. No problem. Maine is the land of easygoing, reasonable compromises. Commit these guidelines to memory, follow to the letter those that particularly strike your fancy, and you'll do just fine.

Right Turn Blinker...

In the Other 49 States
"I am turning right."

In Maine
"I am turning left."

Left Turn Blinker...

"In the Other 49 States
"I am turning left."

In Maine
"I am turning right."

Arm Extended Out Driver's Window...

In the Other 49 States
"I am turning left."

In Maine
"Jeez, deah, look at the hard-on that horse has."

Arm Extended Out Driver's Window, Forearm Pointed Skywards...

In the Other 49 States
"I am turning right."

In Maine
"Look at that fish hawk. Let's shoot it!"

4-Way Flashers on . . .

In the Other 49 States
"I am stopped."

In Maine
"I can't find the cigarette lighter."

Blinking the Headlights . . .

In the Other 49 States
"Please get out of the passing lane."

In Maine
"Oh, there's the cigarette lighter."

Quick Blasts on the Horn . . .

In the Other 49 States
"Get going, you stupid *&*%$!"

In Maine
"I just woke up!"

Motioning with Hand . . .

In the Other 49 States
"Go ahead."

In Maine
"I am cleaning the wax out of my ears."

Pulled Over to the Side of the Road . . .

In the Other 49 States
"I'm parked (safe to pass me)."

In Maine
"I plan to pull out right in front of you and proceed at 10 mph."

Going Extremely Slow . . .

In the Other 49 States
"I'm looking for some particular place."

In Maine
"I know but I won't tell you."

Going Extremely Fast . . .

In the Other 49 States
"I'm in a hurry."

In Maine
"I am senile."

Stopping Suddenly

In the Other 49 States
"I am avoiding hitting something."

In Maine
"Oh, no special reason . . ."

Erratic Steering . . .

In the Other 49 States
"I'm skunk drunk."

In Maine
"Damn, I need a beer . . ."

Who It Pays to Collide with Or, Telling the Different Social Classes by Their Cars.

In order of acceptability, here are the kinds of people you want to run into:

1. People driving 1960 Ford station wagons in mint condition.

Full speed ahead when you sight this kind. They are the Summer Rich and are L-O-A-D-E-D. And if there's a woman in the car, about 55, who still possesses a girlish figure but with a face resembling in texture (from too much sailing) the old workboots you just threw out, they are D-O-U-B-L-E L-O-A-D-E-D. If you're clever, you won't even bother with the insurance companies. Simply offer to pick up some of the glass and ask for a tip.

2. Elderly people driving American-made four-doors dating from the '70s, also in mint condition (the cars, not the people).

Such drivers are Natives and aren't loaded. But they do tend to own valuable things like waterfront property on Penobscot Bay which their grandparents left them free and clear of bank mortgages. Definitely worth squeezing. This may be your only chance to get shorefront acreage. (Tip: Hire a local lawyer to palaver, thunk his suspenders, and generally make the jury forget that you're probably just another out-of-state carpetbagger.)

3. *Suburban types in newish BMWs, Saabs, Peugeots, etc.*

These are yuppies. Maine yuppies, like yuppies elsewhere, can be deceiving. Some have $$$; most of them spend all they have on gourmet cat food. But it may be worth your while to get hit by one—though, personally speaking, we'd steer clear of the ones with those stupid yellow signs in the window which say their 1.2 children are on board. Both of them might very well be lawyers.

4. *People in Japanese cars of any vintage.*

You know how you throw back fish that are too small? Same principle here. The best you can hope for is some typing-pool trainee or a Ph.D. from one of the colleges. Either way, not worth hitting.

5. *Pick-up-truck types.*

Forget car insurance. Think health insurance. When they're done pounding on you, you'll need it. A possible exception is the occasional yuppie who wanted a truck over a jeep because it was more macho and Maine-like. But these people generally do not rise to positions of great importance or income—perhaps because of the difficulty business organizations have in taking seriously anybody who goes to work wearing a cowboy hat with green plastic feathers.

6, 7, 8, 9, 10. *Beat-up old cars; 18-wheel tractor trailers; bikers; any kind of vehicle with a gun rack in the back window; old VW vans.*

Are you kidding?

"Say, how many cord d'you burn last ye-ah?"

"Do you have anything that says independent, rugged yet possessing a certain indefinably gentle strength in size 7½?"

"What do you mean it doesn't get any better than this?"

The Official Maine Values, Attitude, and Lifestyle Survey

Recently the Maine state government commissioned a comprehensive research program to ascertain how the people of Maine stand demographically, economically, and attitudinally in comparison with people in the other states. By utilizing the most state-of-the-art methods of data extrapolation, such as outright lying, consulting the entrails of dead chickens, and calling the Operator when really stuck, the researchers succeeded in compiling the most extensive, authoritative examination ever attempted of this fascinating and often perplexing region. For your free autographed copy of the complete report, send to the publisher five unsoiled labels of your favorite bug juice and explain in twenty-five words or less why you feel that Maine was actually settled thirty-seven years ago by an extraterrestrial civilization. Here is a summary of the report:

Part I: Background demographics

Population:
- living 70%
- deceased 10%
- undecided 20%

Population breakdown:
- a) native 70%
  - born here 50%
  - born again 10%
  - none of your damn business 10%
- b) out-of-state interlopers 30%
  - long-time summer folk who know their place 10%
  - know-it-all New Yorkers who'll get theirs soon enough 10%
  - aging hippies who grow toe-food 10%

Age breakdown:
- 0-18 years 15%
- 19-90 years 50%
- lost count 5%
- can't count 30%

Sex:
- male 50%
- female 50%
- not enough 70%

Part II: Lifestyle analysis

Comparative household income:
- personal income equal to or greater than Switzerland's 15%
- qualifying for Equador's foreign aid 75%
- shove your money, you corporate pigs 10%

Employment picture:
- blue collar 25%
- white collar 10%
- polyester collar 35%
- dog collar 30%

Residence:
- own 40%
- rent 40%
- squat 10%
- torch 10%

Car:
- domestic 50%
- foreign 25%
- home-made 25%

Primary leisure activity:
- watching television 70%
- stealing televisions 5%
- trying to have a child by a BMW 10%
- demonstrating against the war in Vietnam 15%

Secondary leisure activity:
- reading great works of Maine literature like this 5%
- writing great works of Maine literature like this 95%

Part III: Hopes, fears, concerns, favorite Portland restaurant, etc.

"I feel basically optimistic about America's future overall . . ."
- agree strongly 55%
- agree slightly 25%
- never been there 20%

"The greatest problem facing the world today is . . ."
- cheap Canadian imported potatoes 25%
- a shortage of Saab mechanics 10%
- people who mumble to themselves in public 60%
- people who don't mumble 5%

"Maine is a good place to live because there's no street crime."
- agree strongly 80%
- agree slightly 10%
- what's a street? 10%

"I am currently extremely involved with . . ."
- being richer than my friends in Boston 1%
- the anti-nuclear, ecological, and other movements 10%
- my neighbor's wife (husband) 29%
- setting the *Guiness Book of Records* world record for fish calling 60%

"Local government should actively promote..."
- better schools 30%
- worse schools 60%
- what's a school? 10%

"Local government should stamp out..."
- everybody who has more money 85%
- everybody who has less money 10%
- everybody period 5%

"More than anything I want my kids to have..."
- a condo 35%
- my braille deer-hunting license 10%
- a pet tourist 55%

"I'd consider leaving Maine if I could be sure that..."
- I could still weave George McGovern T-shirts 25%
- they had outhouses in Westchester County 45%
- the city people wouldn't bite me 30%

From *The Collectors' Souvenir Edition of Maine Pornography*...

Again and again his angry, iron-hard peevee attacked. The wet, heaving mass surged upwards to meet his pulsing, insistent thrusts. "Take it! Take it! Takeit! Takeit! Takeit!" he panted. The quivering, shuddering, insatiable crotch groaned for more until his seemingly inexhaustible fury had spent itself.

He lit a cigarette, and . . .

(Please turn to page 62.)

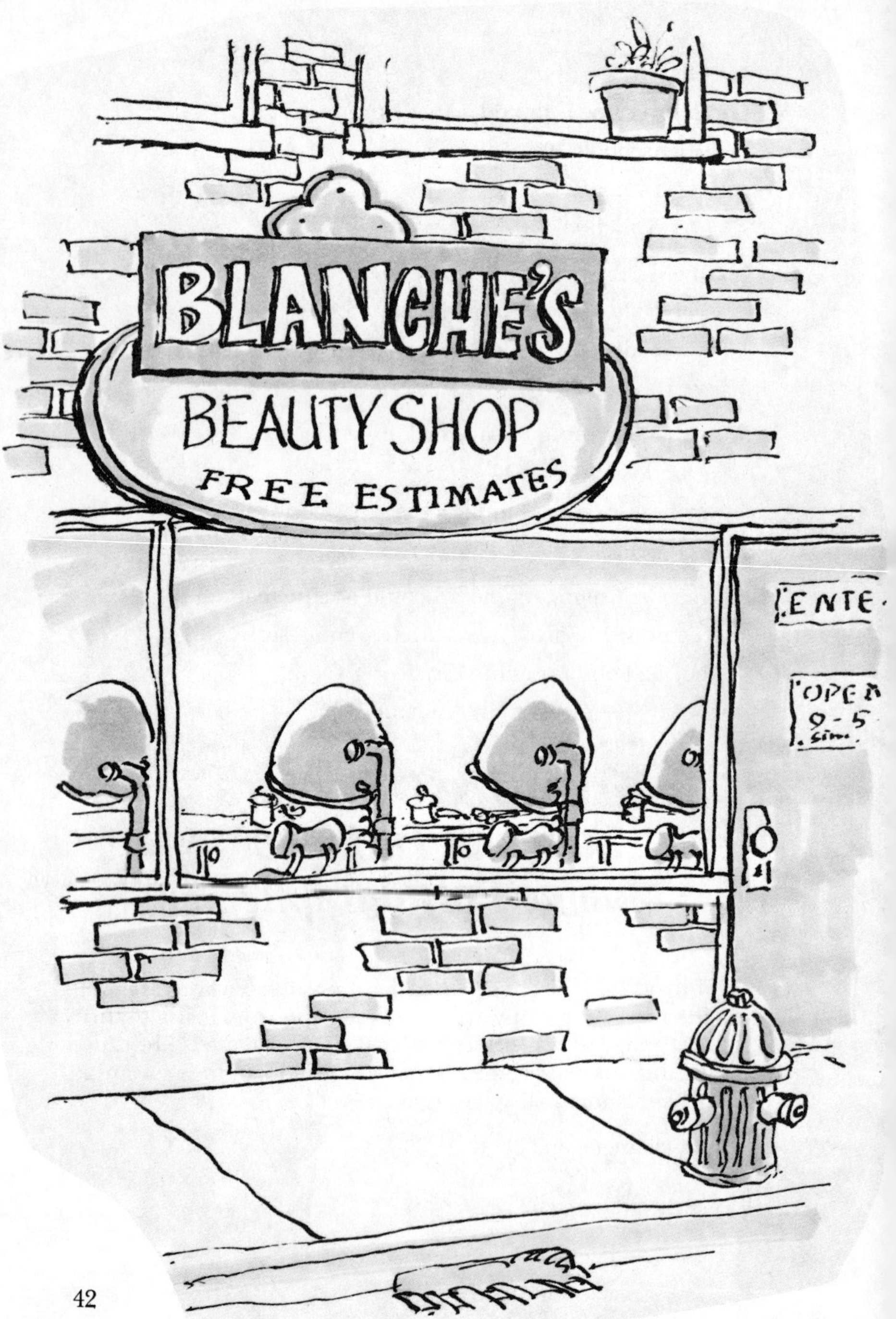
BLANCHE'S
BEAUTY SHOP
FREE ESTIMATES
ENTE
OPE
9 - 5

"These are the Harrisons. They've just moved here from New York."

"Excuse me, would you know how to fix a carburetor?"

"I believe it attracts a more upscale consumer."

Have You Been Paying Attention?

Your Mid-Book Reading Comprehension Exam

Read each question slowly. If you encounter something that makes any sense at all to you, you should reread it carefully. While most of the questions have been drawn from material already covered in the book, some questions haven't anything to do with the preceding material, and others are incredibly irrelevant, not to mention inane. Answers available from the publisher for the sum of $5.00. The publisher reserves the right to change the answers without notice anytime he gets bored.

True/false? Maine played only a limited role in the Italian Renaissance.

True/false? Traditionally the weather has had a much less profound influence on the so-called "Maine" character than have electric outlets.

True/false? The only wood-burning personal computers in the world are manufactured in Portland, Maine.

Pick one. One big thing Maine people have going for them is their incredible...
a. spirit.
b. snowblowing.
c. forty-foot replica of Paul Bunyan.

Choose one. The only thing preventing Maine from becoming a great and prosperous state is the residents' pervasive suspicion of:
a. strangers.
b. flush toilets.
c. movies which give out special glasses.

Translate into good, idiomatic Maine dialect: "The essential pathological lesion in obstructive emphysema is the loss of elasticity and rupture of the aevoli."

Translate into good, idiomatic Maine dialect: "Ultra-Cut-ie Asian singles desire romance! Sncr, gd lkng, cltrd. Order yours by videotape. Box XXX, Grossville, CA."

The following is perhaps the most famous Maine tall tale of them all: "Farmer Perkins' Prize Cow and the Traveling Electric Garter Salesman," as told in authentic Maine dialect. Translate into standard English.

Whallyouey erfiunnmne n' iu mau erurofpmmmm. Uern eur ueo euioln, n' euhf yasgs. Neubytt sayuhhhmm.

"Zaawety, FamammaPehuns, yarbew nmmeupohon?"

"Ayuhneny."

"Qeynammy eunw dizyyet?"

"Ayahneny."

"Whartheyg eybf, aiug!?"

"Ihnuernln melnlmkoij ummemmopmmm mekyunf!!"

Granola Eaters
Imported Upscale
Cheap starchy filler
MEL'S
SKOWHEGAN
SUPERE

"You're right, the little light does stay on."

"Gimme three dough boys and a Diet Coke, please."

Maine Department of Corrections

Authentic Down-Home, Down-East Parlor Games You Can Play with Your Family, Your Friends, and Even Your Enemies

Skowhegan Poker

Arrange as many chairs as you have players in a circle. Deal out from a deck of cards until everybody has some. The first player takes a card at random from his hand and throws it down in the middle of the circle. The other players do likewise until all the cards are gone. They are then gathered up again, and the procedure is repeated. This goes on and on until there is only one player left who hasn't dozed off. This player is declared the winner.

Leaf Racing

A traditional Maine autumn pastime which is best commenced during daylight. The players look out the window and mutually agree upon an acceptable tree. Each player then points out to the other players a leaf which hasn't fallen yet. This leaf becomes "his" leaf. Bets are then placed as to which of the leaves will fall the first, second, third, and so on. Be warned. This is not one of those Slam! Bang! video-type games which are all over in a few seconds. A Maine leaf race can easily last six or seven weeks, particularly if the weather is mild.

Alphabetic Brain Twisters

One player is selected as "It" and is given a bucket of water to put upon his head. He announces to the others that he is thinking of some word with such and such a letter in it, but that he isn't sure exactly which word he is thinking of. The other players must tell him which word he is trying to think of. The first one to propose a word whose meaning both players know gets to take the bucket and fling it against the wall, shouting: "Water, water on the brain, sell the cat and take the train!" Recommended for players 21 years and older.

78 rpm Hoe-Down

This is the true Mainer's answer to the old-fashioned square dance. You will need an old record player, preferably a Victrola, but on certain kinds of tape decks you can run tapes at different speeds, which will also be OK. Next, you and your friends gather together all your favorite new records and play them at 78 rpm. And when that gets boring you can take turns spinning them backwards with your finger and singing along.

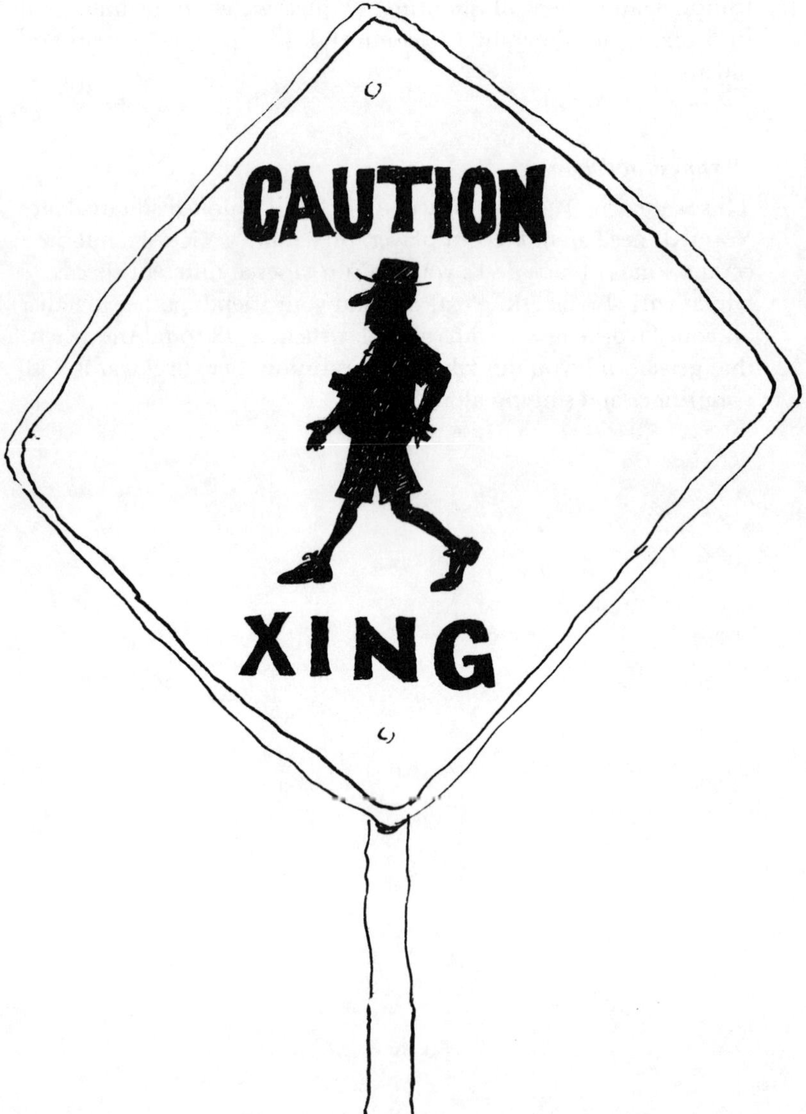
CAUTION
XING

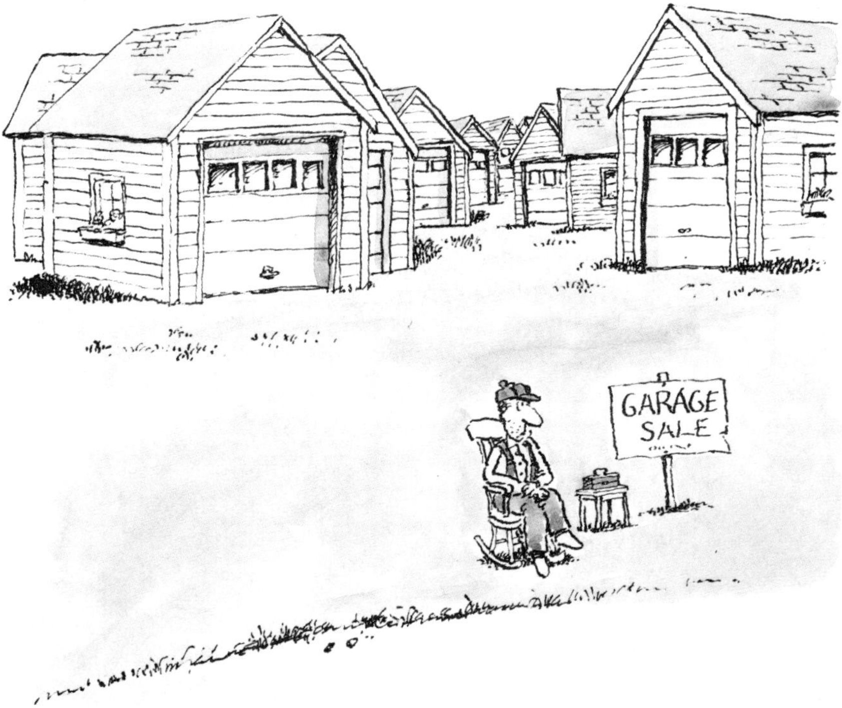
GARAGE
SALE

Beginning of the ad campaign

...and I think, gentlemen, you'll agree that we've simply but eloquently captured the essence of the proud, noble heritage of whatever the hell it is you people do up here."

End of the ad campaign

"On the other hand, gentlemen, when you turn the chart this way, it reveals an entirely different picture."

Sailing the Maine Coast

What to See, What to Do, How to Tell When You're There

Portsmouth, N.H., to Portland

This smooth, straight section is called the southern coast because of its strong resemblance to parts of Florida. You can navigate it easily with a route map from any filling station.

Portland/Casco Bay

A helpful landmark for boats approaching Portland used to be the time and temperature sign high atop the second floor of the Savings & Loan & Hardware Building. This authentic marvel of the twentieth century consists of thirty lightbulbs which flash on in different combinations, telling at a glance what time it is and how much money is in the bank. Recently, however, yachtspeople have reported that this friendly beacon is no longer visible owing to a fifteen-story, marble salt-water lavatory which Portland's city fathers erected as a monument to themselves. Casco Bay itself boasts many islands worthy of a visit. They are generally unspoiled, inhabited for the most part by natives who light bonfires to lure passing aircraft bound for Europe to their destruction, and who then scavenge the wrecks.

Boothbay Harbor/The Mid-Coast

Here begin the remote inlets, the silent, fog-shrouded coves, the fabled ports-of-call that have made Maine's coast famous. Boothbay Harbor is particularly noteworthy. In heavy traffic a wise skipper will approach Boothbay by car on State Highway 27.

Muscongus Bay

Anchor at New Improved Harbor. Then take the town taxi out to "Gravity Hill." This is Maine's most inexplicable natural marvel, and a source of amazement and delight to scientists and tourists alike. Follow the only road north out of town until you ascend the first hill. Have the taxi driver shut off the engine at the summit. Then, the taxi still pointed straight ahead, the brakes are released. As if by magic you'll find yourself and the taxi both transported to the bottom of the hill . . . definitely bring your camera, and film, too!

Monhegan Island

This storm-battered strip of land has defied the elements since it was erected half a century ago during the FDR New Deal years. Transported in huge sections from a quarry in Allentown, Pennsylvania, and deposited by hand over ten miles out at sea, Monhegan remains the C.C.C.'s most ambitious public-works project, although the electric and plumbing systems were never completed because the Depression was declared over shortly after the island was launched. Travelers' hint: The island is shut down for a week in September to enable the state's maintenance crews to repaint the scenery.

Mt. Desert Island

The state health authorities had much of this region burned back in the '40s. However, it is now perfectly safe to visit for short periods. Contrary to what even the latest government charts suggest, Mt. Desert Island is *not* at the edge of the globe. However, expeditions returning from the one filling station in New Brunswick have reported that the people living there have one eye, tails of serpents, and worship seaweed. They are also said to give gold and silver in exchange for old sunglasses.

"You and your 'let's eat where the natives eat.'"

"I said, the philosopher Schopenhauer, in his seminal investigations into the metaphysical foundations of conduct, decisively proved for once and all the existence of a higher ontological reality, and any plain damn fool knows that. Ten Fowah..."

From *The Collectors' Souvenir Edition of Maine Pornography* ...

Continued from page 41

... studied the river still swollen from the rains. His tool now lay lifeless in his hands as, defeated, he exhaled the smoke slowly. "Hell! It's a bitch breakin' up a goddamn log jam!"

"Distinguished citizens of Earth... Having followed the progress of your civilization from afar, it is in friendship not unmixed with feelings of profound pleasure that we now judge your planet ready to take its rightful—and if I may say, long-awaited—place on the supreme legislative council of the galaxy, and so we have come today in order to bestow full and equal membership with all rights, privileges, prerogatives..."

A Rainy Day in Maine

Or, 8 Great New Ways to Amuse Yourself with a Paper Clip

"If I were as rich as the richest king on earth, gladly would I exchange it all for a day in which I could experience once more the silent, gray, epic beauty that is uniquely the Maine coast's in a seven-day fog."

—Homer Baxter Pebble

Editor's Note: Interested persons may call, visit, or write Mr. Pebble care of The Maine Home for the Totally Insane, Augusta, Maine.

1. Place a personal ad on the paper clip's behalf.

Think of how many appealing things you can say about it (Non-smoking, Single, Straight, Slender, Quiet, Strong Silent Type . . .) without, strictly speaking, telling a lie. Don't forget to mention in your ad that all replies will be answered and a photo will be enclosed.

2. Gourmet tasting session.

So you and your friends really think you know your clips, eh? Well, try the blindfold test. For serving suggestions, consult last week's issue of *The American Journal of Metallurgy*.

3. Start a religion in which it is the Supreme Being.

Take turns seeing how many people you can convert! Winner gets to wear a turban and own fifteen Rolls Royces.

4. Group voodoo.

Bend as many clips as you need so that they look more or less like people and name each after one of your enemies. Don't be afraid to bear grudges; a whole box costs only 39 cents. Then use your chain saw . . . a grindstone . . . a cooking pot. Enjoy! Enjoy! Nobody's been burned in Maine for witchcraft in over thirty-five years.

5. *Parents special.*

At the dinner table with your kids, adamantly insist that they're vegetables (the clips), and bully your kids until they eat them all. Remember that you can bend paper clips to cunningly resemble asparagus, broccoli, spinach, potatoes or whatever!

6. *Leave everything you own to one.*

Get on the phone. Call your lawyer. Disinherit everybody. Don't forget to mention that you're in sound mind and body, or your little joke won't work.

7. *Secret forbidden games of sex and bizarre procreation.*

Invite up your simpy-liberal sister from Boston for the weekend and introduce her to a person of a different molecular structure.

8. *A last resort.*

For when you're hard up . . . really, really hard up. Get yourself an airline ticket to Washington, D.C., bring along a clip, make an appointment at the Pentagon, show it around, come back to Maine with $50,000, and spill another $4.95 on another one of our books.

Maine Body Language

State of relaxation   *State of affection*

State of irritation   *State of elation*

What Color Are Your Food Stamps?

How to Find Valuable and Rewarding Professional Careers in Maine with a $39.95 Metal Detector

Note: To do this exercise you will need some colored markers; an 8½" x 11" pad of yellow, lined paper; a Maine telephone book, including the white and yellow pages; and at least two family trust funds.

Previous accomplishments inventory
1. Write down everything you've ever done which you consider valuable or rewarding or professionally satisfying at any point during your education or in previous jobs.
2. Crumple up your list into a fairly tight ball and set fire to it next winter to stay warm.

Get to know the local movers and shakers in your chosen field
If you happen not to have a field, don't worry. A backyard will do. So will an old Maine farmhouse attic crawl space, provided it allows enough space to move and shake in.

Unemployment really works!
They can't make you take a job outside of your chosen profession. So, if you were a corporation lawyer, a computer engineer, a brain surgeon, an advertising executive, or anything like that back in The Real World, you can just sit back and collect. You don't even have to go through the pretense of looking. See the last paragraph in this chapter about what to do when your benefits run out.

The interview
Show up well in advance. All the other people also looking for work will have to line up behind you. On the other hand, don't

seem too eager—the employer might think you're not from Maine. And don't ever, ever commit the *faux pas* of one CPA from Boston interviewing for an entry-level position with a large fish-processing corporation Down East. He put on his résumé that he once had a summer job shoveling fish heads in St. Tropez. Maine employers mistrust employees with a history of taking vacations.

What is a good salary in Maine?

Anything that leaves enough left over to see a movie every other leap year. Also, savvy job seekers don't hesitate to raise the subject of perks themselves, offering prospective companies their car, their spouse, their brothers and sisters, their children, even their memberships in the local A.A. chapter.

Interim work

Definitely! And if you can't find any, follow the example of many resourceful newcomers who invent causes to become head of: The Farmyard Animals' Rape Crisis Center . . . Clergy and Laity Opposed to Central Heating . . . Emergency Coalition to Outlaw Concerned Citizens . . . People Against Wasting Paper for Bumper Stickers . . .

"We picked it up from one of the natives for virtually a song."

Who Makes What in Maine

Accountant, CPA

Everywhere else
$80,000+

In Maine
$27.98. More if you're experienced in the area of bottle-return transactions.

Advertising Executive

Everywhere else
$70,000-250,000

In Maine
Barter system. As a rule of thumb, one basket of fresh-caught fish equals one advertising campaign.

Banker

Everywhere else
$90,000-300,000

In Maine
Free haircuts at the local barber shop.

Brain Surgeon

Everywhere else
$110,000-200,000

In Maine
Piece work. Business can be very slow in some counties.

Doctor, G.P.

Everywhere else
$100,000-150,000

In Maine
See Advertising Executive and multiply by two.

Engineer, High-Tech

Everywhere else
$50,000-130,000

In Maine
Huh?

Lawyer

Everywhere else
$50,000-400,000

In Maine
12¢ a dozen.

TV Anchor Personality

Everywhere else
$200,000-600,000

In Maine
Depends on the proceeds from their part-time paper route.

"He says you can't get there from here."

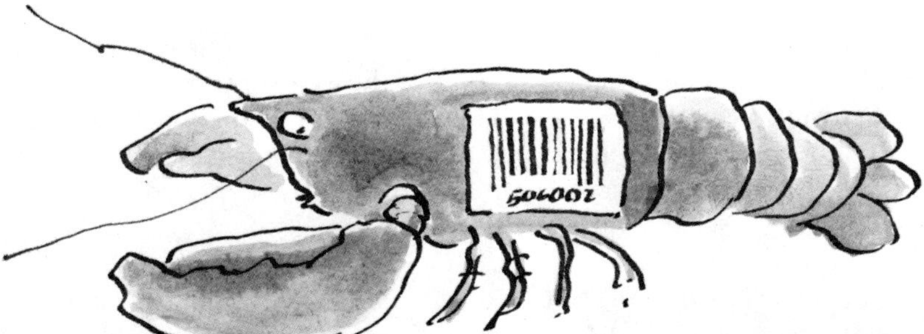

Arts Diary

A Sensitive New Hampshire Critic Tours the Maine Arts Scene.

Day one: Portsmouth, N.H. Attended a gallery reception featuring a celebrated Maine artist from Livermore Falls. This artist had a bunch of televisions lined up which were all showing various quiz shows. He stood there facing them like an orchestra conductor. When a contestant got a question wrong, he blew the set away with a sawed-off shotgun. I wonder how I'm going to like Maine art! It's so *direct!*

Day two: Ogunquit There is talk of moving the entire town up to the Canadian border to take some of the tourist pressure off the South Coast. The biggest gallery, The Rive Gauche Trading Post, had an exhibit called "A Celebration of Things 30% Off." Bought a series of black-and-white photographs of "period" inner tubes. What a find!

Day three: Portland The Cheap Thrills Theatre Troupe put on a one-act play about the interrelationships and familial bonds among a pile of rocks. A couple in the next row talked through the whole thing, which was o.k, since the rocks didn't. So avant-garde!

Day four: Bath Televised live on the statewide public broadcasting station: a college professor lecturing on the existential philosophical implications of "Leave It to Beaver." Townies in the audience got bored and pelted him with empty beer cans. The show's producer told me the station redeems the cans. It's the novel way they've invented to raise money, which, he said, is hard to come by in this state.

Day five: Camden   Got sick of hearing Mozart performed on two saws, a washboard and box springs, so walked out on a performance of the Presque Isle String Quartet. However, also going on in town: A local mime company held a benefit performance on behalf of themselves. And there was a male/female act doing an incredible portrayal of a shy man courting a bowl of soup. Not a dry eye in the house!

Day Six: Bar Harbor   Contra dance at The Church of The Good Riddance. Somebody got up and sang a hundred and forty-five verses of a lovely, traditional Down East ballad. When will New Hampshire ever get to have such a well-developed arts scene?

"I moved to Maine when I got fed up with the pseudo-glamorous Big City lifestyle with its bogus rewards and incentives, and could no longer find personal fulfillment in an environment which I had come to realize was fundamentally insane and meaningless... and I could really go for another Martini Rossi, how 'bout you?"

Examples of Acceptable and Unacceptable Names for Maine People

Acceptable

Male Names	Female Names
Bup	Wen
Bone	Licorice
Bangor	Feasibility
Dubba	Vendetta

Unacceptable

Male Names	Female Names
Rip	Wendy
Boston	George
Lance	Portland
Tab	Muffy

"In my day we made money the old-fashioned way, we married into it."

"Okay, big trees. Okay, pretty ocean sunset. Okay, rock-bound coast. Now what?"

The Most Important Referendum Question to be Put Before the People of Maine in the History of the World

This is a real, live petition to change the name of the state from "Maine" to something snappier. This form may be duplicated. Distribute extra copies around your neighborhood. If you don't have any neighbors, make up a name and sign it with your left hand or with your foot. Note that all signers must indicate a current, legal residence in the so-called State of Maine. (Non-residents can get around this by signing the registration number of their L.L. Bean's boots.) Send completed form to the DUMP ME ALLIANCE, c/o the publisher.

WHEREAS, the present name of the state, "Maine," is a second-hand name in that whoever discovered this place named it after some poverty-stricken place back in France that he was reminded of; and

WHEREAS it rhymes with "pain," "drain," "rain," "slain," "plain Jane," not to mention "(chil)blains"; and

WHEREAS these words have highly negative meanings and connotations and probably explain why "Maine" has never hosted an Olympics, a World's Fair, or even a National Fishwives Convention; and

WHEREAS if more tourists came and threw more of their money around maybe someday our per capita income might overtake that of Haiti; and

WHEREAS the science of marketing, product-positioning, and mass-motivation have attained a very high degree of sophistication in The Real World; and

WHEREAS the State Department of Economic Development has commissioned a New York advertising agency to develop another name for the State; and

WHEREAS this new name will communicate all the positive perceptions of the "Maine" experience and will greatly assist promoting them to out-of-state consumers; and

WHEREAS changing its name will enable the State to elude its many creditors, including the aforementioned New York advertising agency;

BE IT RESOLVED THAT THE STATE CHANGE ITS NAME FROM "MAINE" TO "CAP'N ROY'S FUN-O-RAMA,"

which question to be put before the voters of Maine in public and binding referendum, held not later than the first Tuesday in the month of November.

Signed,

Name	Address	County	L.L. Bean Boot Registration Number (if applicable)

"...and what would you like for starch?"

"I grant you it does say 'Maine,' but does it say 'hedge against inflation'?"

Suggestions for Further Reading

The Joy of Rabies, Running Water Press, Presque Isle ME. A heartwarming classic of a boy and his dog in a turn-of-the-century rural Maine town, delightfully told by the doctor who shot them.

On a Clear Day You Can See Your Feet, Vision Press, Dark Harbor ME. The ultimate guide to Maine weather in all its many, varied, eye-catching shades of gray. Profusely illustrated with over forty-five perfectly opaque color plates.

Consumer's Update Reviews Maine Humor, Jonathan Bile Books, Trenton NJ. "You can't get there from here . . .," "Well I know I ain't lost . . .," "25,000 miles the way you're goin' . . ." Just how funny are they? And all those baked-bean supper jokes—are they Down East or Far East? There's strong evidence that these old favorites are actually cheap soybean imports cooked up in Taiwan! Plus 30-page Special Insert: The Great Ayuh Scam.

The Wholistic Automobile Club's Bed and Breakfast Guide to Maine's Cults, Communes and Obscure Religions, Spacy Press, 45 Planetary Drive, Far Out CA. See the Maine most visitors never see, and fewer still return to talk about. Check out such exotic events as Annual Human Sacrifice Baking Contests, the Gypsy Rodeo, the Great Witches' Schooner Race. Also: Maine's many singing-in-tongues folk festivals and white-water yoga gatherings. Affordable, comfortable places to experience rebirth. Local dietary laws and all important taboos are carefully noted as well as establishments which accept benedictions in lieu of life-denying, chemically prepared currency.

In and Out in Maine, Red Light Press, Paris ME. The definitive vacationer's guide to Maine's famous *filles de joie* and various discreet, deluxe resorts catering to the most rarefied tastes. Each establishment graded in terms of services, atmosphere, cleanliness and paraphernalia by means of a convenient 1-4 Scar™ rating system for quick reference. Newly updated sections include Maine's many picturesque gay outlets and inlets.

"I just want to say you're all incredibly beautiful people."

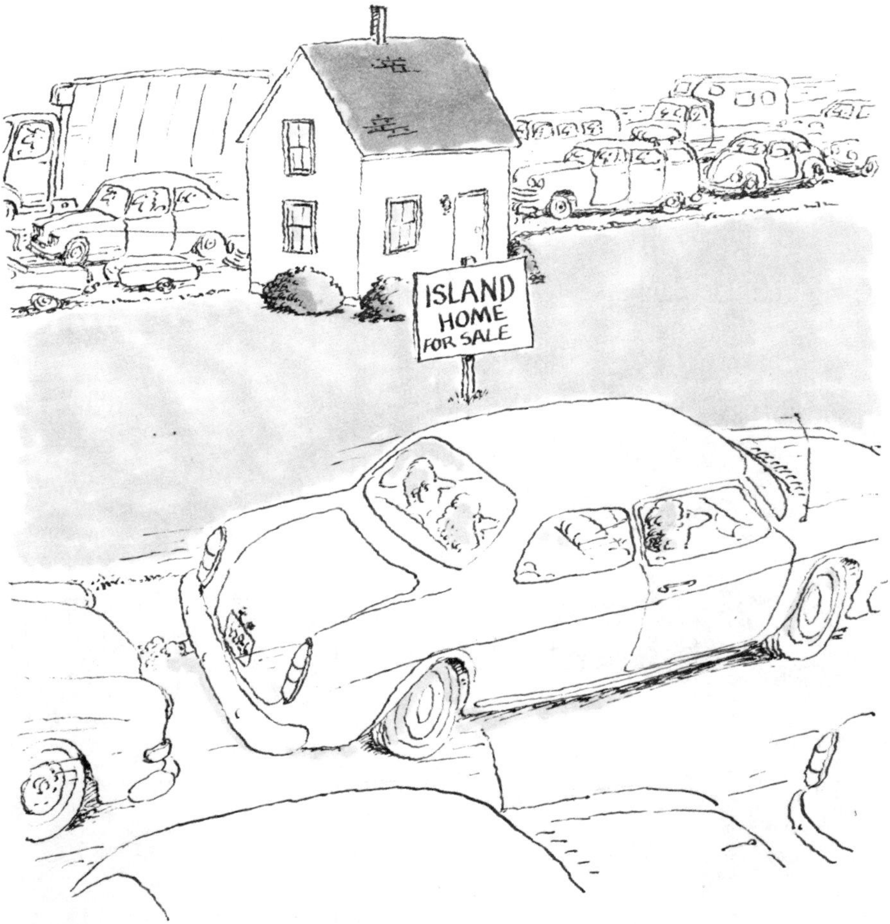
ISLAND
HOME
FOR SALE

"What'll ya gimme for her?"

"There goes the neighborhood."

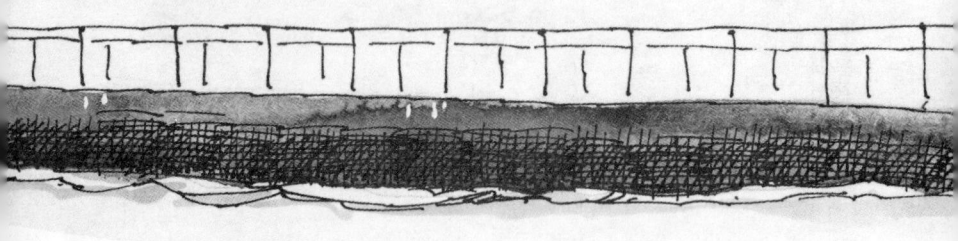

"You're gonna have to throw it back, Vern."